Major League SOCCER

Seattle Sounders

Marty Gitlin

SEATTLE
SOUNDERS FC

Mitchell Lane
PUBLISHERS

2001 SW 31st Avenue
Hallandale, FL 33009

www.mitchelllane.com

Printing   1   2   3   4   5   6   7   8

Designer: Ed Morgan
Editor: Sharon F. Doorasamy

Library of Congress Cataloging-in-Publication Data

Names: Gitlin, Marty, author.
Title: Seattle Sounders FC / by Marty Gitlin.
Description: Hallandale, FL : Mitchell Lane Publishers, 2018. | Series: Major League Soccer |
   Includes bibliographical references and index.
Identifiers: LCCN 2018003132| ISBN 9781680202649 (library bound) | ISBN 9781680202656 (ebook)
Subjects: LCSH: Seattle Sounders FC (Soccer team)—History—Juvenile literature.
Classification: LCC GV943.6.S43 G58 2018 | DDC 796.334/6409797772—dc23
LC record available at https://lccn.loc.gov/2018003132

Contents

Words in **bold** throughout can be found in the Glossary.

All About MLS

The United States is unique in its passion for sports. The most popular among Americans are football, baseball, and basketball. The favorite in most of the world is soccer. That sport is played by more than 265 million people in 200 nations.

But the number of soccer fans and players in the United States has grown since the 1990s. Youth leagues sprang up around the country as kids began to embrace the game. More people started watching international matches on television. Soccer in the United States received a boost in 1994. That is when the country gained the opportunity to host the FIFA World Cup for the first time.

FIFA stands for the Federation Internationale de Football Association. The organization runs the sport worldwide. And it demanded that a professional soccer league be launched in the United States to earn the right to host the World Cup.

The result was Major League Soccer (MLS). It opened play with 10 **franchises** in 1996. Not every major city in the United States boasted a team. Even the huge city of Chicago did not have a franchise.

An impressive average of 17,406 fans attended MLS games in its first season and the number continued to grow. It rose by about 5,000 over the next five years and peaked at 21,692 in 2016. The most successful franchise proved to be the Seattle Sounders, which averaged more than 40,000 fans per game during that period.

Chapter One

The league continued to expand. It reached 22 teams in 2017, all but three of which reside in the United States. The Canadian cities of Montreal, Toronto, and Vancouver had also gained franchises. The MLS is divided into an Eastern Conference and Western Conference of 11 teams each.

Among the most positive aspects of Major League Soccer is its **diversity**. Nearly half of all its players in 2015 were born outside of the United States and Canada. But the league boasted more American players than those of any other country. California alone produced a whopping 57 players, with Texas next at 27.

Each MLS team receives three points for every victory and one for a tie. They all seek to earn a spot in the playoffs by placing among the top six in their conference. The two teams that tally the most points in each conference receive a **bye** in the first round of the **playoffs**. That allows those teams to advance to the next round while the other teams must win a match to remain alive.

The following two rounds are two-match playoffs. The teams that score the most goals in those two matches play for the **MLS Cup** championship in December.

It is a long season. Nine months pass from the first match to the final match. But the wait and work are worth it, especially for the team that takes the title.

Fun Facts

1 MLS players spend plenty of time on planes. Those that compete for teams in the Northwest travel especially long distances to matches. In 2016, the Portland, Oregon, and Seattle, Washington, teams both flew more than 40,000 miles.

2 One complaint about soccer among American fans is its low-scoring matches. Teams rarely score more than three goals. But it does happen—even in the MLS Cup finals. San Jose tallied four goals in 2003 to beat Chicago in the title match.

Greatness from the Start

The date was March 19, 2009. More than 30,000 fans streamed into Qwest Field in Seattle. The Sounders were set to play their first Major League Soccer match. Excitement was in the air.

A hero emerged that night. His name was Fredy Montero. And his MLS debut took the city by storm. The **Colombian** forward blasted the ball past New York goalkeeper Danny Cepero for the first goal in Sounders history. He recorded their first assist minutes later. Montero then placed the cherry on top of a sweet victory. He faked out Cepero and booted the ball into the net to cap the 3–0 win.

Fredy Montero (*center*) receives a pass from teammate Brad Evans (*right*) in the opening match at Qwest Field March 19, 2009, in Seattle, Washington.

Few expected much from the Sounders that season. After all, they were a first-year franchise. **Expansion** teams in all sports usually struggle. They most often do not boast the talent to win. But the Sounders had signed many top players. They finished the season with a 12–7 record to earn a playoff spot. They did it with defense. They led the league with just 29 goals allowed.

The Sounders took their momentum and ran with it. They won the Lamar Hunt U.S. Open Cup in each of their first three years. They reached the Major League Soccer playoffs every season through 2016. They topped the MLS with 56 goals scored in 2011. They allowed the fewest goals in 2012 and 2014.

And the fans came out in droves. The Sounders have achieved the highest **attendance** in Major League Soccer every year through 2016. They have averaged more than 40,000 fans per home game since 2009. Their average of 42,636 in 2016 is the best in league history.

The fans feel loyal to a team that is loyal to Seattle. Even the team name and colors reflect the area. The Sounders are connected to a city that sits on the shores of the **Puget Sound**. The blue in the uniform signifies the bodies of water that surround the city. The green represents the forests of the Pacific Northwest.

It is no wonder that the Sounders attract about twice as many fans as many teams in the league. They pack what is known as CenturyLink Field. Yet those same fans became frustrated after a few seasons. Their favorite team faded in the playoffs every year.

CentryLink Field in 2012

Chapter Two

The most painful defeats occurred in 2014. The Sounders finished with the best record in the league. They earned their first MLS Supporters' Shield. That is awarded to the team that scores the most points during the regular season. They even won their fourth U.S. Open Cup.

The Sounders reached the Western Conference finals of the MLS Cup. They even beat the Los Angeles Galaxy in the second match of that round. But they failed to advance because the Galaxy scored the only goal in a road match. The Sounders had still not played for a championship.

Then came 2016. The Sounders won just half of their games that year. But they eked into the playoffs. They then steamrolled past three Western Conference rivals into the MLS Cup finals against the Toronto FC. The defenses dominated as the two teams battled for the crown. They played 90 scoreless minutes. An overtime of 30 minutes passed without a score.

The title would come down to penalty kicks. The **shootout** was tied at 4–4. The outcome rested on the strong right leg of Seattle defender Roman Torres. Toronto goalkeeper Clint Irwin guessed that Torres would kick the ball to the right. But Torres blasted it to the left into the net. The Sounders had captured their first MLS title!

Torres sprinted across the field. He was mobbed by his teammates. The fans in Toronto sat in stunned silence. But there were enough Sounders fans in the stands to let out a loud roar. They were proud of their Sounders. And they were thrilled to be fans of a championship team.

Roman Torres (*left*) celebrates his championship winning goal against the Toronto FC in the 2016 MLS Cup on December 10, 2016, in Toronto, Canada.

Fun Facts

1 One of the Sounders's four owners is Drew Carey. Carey is a very funny actor and comedian. He is also host of legendary television game show called *The Price is Right*. He gained an interest in soccer while attending a Galaxy match in 2003.

2 Spanish soccer team FC Barcelona never performed in front of a bigger crowd than it did on August 5, 2009. That is when it played the Sounders in an exhibition match in Seattle. The battle attracted 66,848 fans at CenturyLink Field. Soccer superstar Lionel Messi scored two goals as Barcelona won the match, 4–0.

How the Game is Played

Imagine you are a goalkeeper in Major League Soccer. You are all alone. And the team is depending on you. You must stop booted balls from landing in the net. You know that one goal can mean defeat. After all, many MLS matches end in a 1–0 score.

You are lonely out there. Sometimes you even feel nervous. But you get plenty of help from defenders. Their job is to prevent shots on goal. They try to steal the ball or kick it away from opponents.

The first line of defense are the three midfielders and two wingbacks. The midfielders are aptly named because they play around midfield. The wingbacks also play close to the center line. But they roam around the sidelines.

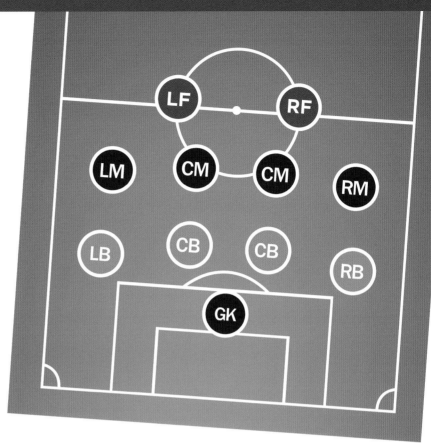

Goalkeeper(GK)
Right back defender (RB)
Left back defender (LB)
Center back defender (CB)
Left midfielder (LM)
Center midfielder (CM)
Right midfielder (RM)
Left forward (LF)
Right forward (RF)

The goalkeeper has four other defenders closer to him. They are the fullbacks and center-backs. The two fullbacks also defend near the sidelines. The two center-backs play the middle.

Everyone else on the field has at least some offensive tasks. Two center midfielders play both offense and defense. The attacking midfielder tries to control and pass the ball to set up scores.

Wings and forwards play closest to the goal. They seek to boot the ball into the net. They sometimes even slam the ball off their heads past goalkeepers. Those shots are called headers.

The forwards grab the spotlight because they score the most goals. But every player on the field is vital to success.

Chapter Three

The teams with the best talent win games and championships. They also create **rivalries** against other top teams. Major League Soccer boasts many heated rivalries. Some are based on great playoff matches in the past. Other teams become rivals because their cities are located nearby.

Perhaps the most intense MLS rivalry is between Seattle and the Portland Timbers. Both teams reside in the northwest United States. Seattle has also developed a rivalry against Los Angeles. The Galaxy holds the record for most league titles with five. But the Sounders earned the crown in 2016.

Other MLS rivalries are based on long histories. Among the best is D.C. United against New York. They have been Eastern Conference rivals since the MLS began in 1996.

Darlington Nagbe (*left*) with Tyrone Mears (*right*) and Chad Marshall during a Seattle Sounders versus Portland Timbers game in Portland, Oregon.

Rivalries attract fans to matches. Such fan support often helps players perform well. The Sounders owned a better home record every year but 2011. Their mark at CenturyLink Field since 2009 is an incredible 78–29. But they have lost more than half of their games on the road.

Major Soccer League players find it hard to perform their best away from home. Long plane travel and living out of hotels can sap energy. And cheering fans bring energy to their opponents. Even teams with less talent often win most of their home games.

Home fans have certainly helped Seattle win matches. But the Sounders have also boasted great players. They have never been saddled with a losing record. They have proven to be one of the winningest franchises in American sports since joining MLS in 2009.

The Sounders snagged the crown in 2016. Did that signal a **dynasty** that will result in more titles? Only time will tell.

Fun Facts

1 The Sounders played quite well on the road from 2009 to 2014. They sported a 37–34 mark away from home during that time. Their 9–3 mark in 2011 was the best in the league. They stumbled to a 4–9 road record in each of the next two years. Yet they won the MLS championship in 2016.

2 The green and blue Sounders logo features the Space Needle in the center. The Space Needle is Seattle's most famous landmark. It is an observation tower that hovers 605 feet over the city. The Space Needle was built in 1962.

Best of the Best

Time was running out in the 2012 Western Conference semifinals. Seattle and Real Salt Lake remained scoreless. Someone had to play the role of hero.

That someone was Sounders midfielder Mario Martinez.

His team had never won a playoff series. More than 80 minutes had elapsed in the match. Nobody had booted the ball into the net. Martinez worked his way free on the left side of the field. A pass bounced in from Fredy Montero. Martinez wasted no time. He rocketed the ball past diving goalkeeper Nick Rimando into the right corner of the net.

The Sounders celebrated the goal. Soon they were celebrating their first trip to the conference finals.

But Martinez was merely a star of the moment. The Sounders have boasted some of the greatest all-time players in Major League Soccer.

None made a bigger splash then Montero. It was no wonder he was named MLS Newcomer of the Year in 2009. Montero remains the leading scorer in Sounders history with 47 goals in league play. But it was not Montero that earned a spot on the league all-star team in 2009. It was midfielder Freddie Ljungberg.

Ljundberg was the first of five Sounders to be so honored. None was more popular than Kasey Keller. The 2011 all-star goalkeeper hailed from the city of Olympia. That is just an hour drive from Seattle.

Goalkeeper Kasey Keller makes a save on a header shot by Veljko Paunovic (*center*) of the Philadelphia Union with James Riley at CenturyLink Field in October 2011.

Chapter Four

Two top scorers in Sounders history behind Montero also earned first-team status. Midfielder Osvaldo Alonso was awarded in 2012. Forward Obafemi Martins followed two years later. Martins landed on the first team that year along with Seattle defender Chad Marshall. It was no wonder that Seattle boasted two all-stars that season. They finished with the best record in Major League Soccer.

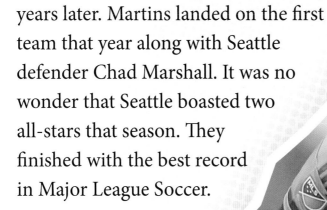

Obafemi Martins controls the ball against the New England Revolution at CenturyLink Field in March 2015.

The most famous Sounders player ever helped the team achieve that best record. But he never earned a spot among the MLS all-stars. That was forward Clint Dempsey. Dempsey signed with Seattle in 2013. He ranked among the greatest players in the United States. It took the largest contract in MLS history to lure him away from the English Premier League.

Dempsey proved his worth. He ranked third behind Montero and Martins among career scorers in Sounders history through 2016. Dempsey and Martins were quite the one-two punch in 2014. They combined for 32 goals to help Seattle achieve the best record in Major League Soccer that season.

Clint Dempsey shoots a goal with a bicycle kick against the San Jose Earthquakes in August 2014.

The oddest and worst regular season ever for the Sounders ended with them jumping for joy over their first championship. The year began with Martins leaving the team to play in China. In July, the Sounders were in danger of not making the playoffs for the first time in franchise history. Head coach Sigi Schmid was fired and replaced by Brian Schmetzer. Soon Dempsey was sidelined with an illness.

But the Sounders overcame all their problems. They began to roll. They lost just two of their last 14 regular season games. They took their momentum and ran with it into the MLS Cup playoffs. Soon Torres was booting the game-winner against Toronto. The Sounders were champions.

Players such as Montero, Keller, and Martins became stars in Seattle. But every player that has worn a Sounders uniform helped them become one of the finest teams in Major League Soccer.

Fun Facts

1 The second-largest crowd in MLS history showed up at CenturyLink Field on August 25, 2013. They came in droves to watch a match between the Sounders and Portland. The rivalry between the two teams is known as the Cascadia Cup. More than 67,000 arrived to see the Sounders win the match, 1–0.

2 Sounder goalkeeper Stefan Frei made the biggest save in team history. He leaped to deflect a shot by Toronto forward Jozy Altidore in overtime of the MLS championship in 2016. The incredible save kept the match scoreless. It allowed the Sounders to capture the crown in a shootout.

Jozy Altidore (*right*) of Toronto FC heads the ball but Stefan Frei makes the save of the MLS Cup Final on December 10, 2016.

A New World

They come from all over the world to grace the rosters of Major League Soccer teams. They arrive from Europe, South America, and Africa. They love that they play an **international** sport.

Some of those who compete in Major League Soccer do not speak English. They have never performed in the United States. They have never visited the cities of the United States. They must adjust to a new world. And it is not easy.

Each MLS teams can carry a roster of 30 players. Only eight can be international. Many of them travel thousands of miles from home. They live in what is to them a strange place. Daily life is much harder than kicking a ball into a net.

They must learn a new language. They are away from their families. They are in a world of strangers. They try to make friends with whom they have nothing in common. They have new teammates and coaches they cannot always understand. They must find a new home. They must learn how to buy things with U.S. money.

Their one comfort zone should be the soccer field. But even playing a familiar sport is harder. They do not know what teammates are saying on the field. They need help to understand commands of their coaches. They cannot answer questions from the media without an **interpreter**.

Travel in the United States and Canada can also be tough. They are two of the largest countries in the world. Foreign players most often come from much smaller nations. They are used to traveling short distances to matches on buses or trains. They must get used to spending hours on planes and sleeping in hotels.

Chapter Five

Major League Soccer teams often play on Saturday nights. But they leave on Thursday or Friday. Matches end late. Players do not return home until Sunday. They often spend four days on the road. That can be easy for American and Canadian players who speak English. It can be brutal for those who do not know the language.

Even the weather can be harsh on foreign players. The weather in smaller countries is often nearly the same from one end to the other. MLS players might have a Wednesday match on a cool evening in Canada. Three days later they could play in the scorching heat of Texas. And a week later they could play in the heavy rains of Portland.

The change on the field goes beyond calling the sport soccer instead of football. Foreign players must **adapt** to a different style. Major League Soccer boasts a faster pace than the sport in other parts of the world. Matches are won with skill and talent.

The best athletes excel in MLS. There is less strategy. Foreign players are often lost on the field until they get used to the speed of the game.

It takes time. But their ability and love for soccer shine through. The greatest players in Sounders are prime examples. Ljungberg came from Sweden. Montero arrived from Colombia. Martins is a native of Nigeria. Alonso played in Cuba before wearing the Seattle uniform. Standout midfielder Alvaro Fernandez is from the South American country of Uruguay.

Those stars have helped make Major League Soccer truly an international league. And they have made the Sounders perhaps the most successful franchise in the league.

Fun Facts

1 Goalkeeper Kasey Keller last played for the Sounders in 2011 before retiring. But he remained close to the team. Keller has since served as an announcer for the Sounders's radio and television broadcasts. He gives expert analysis on the team and the sport.

2 The most famous international player to join an MLS team was David Beckham. He starred in England and Spain before signing a huge contract to play for the Los Angeles Galaxy. Beckham helped his team win the MLS Cup in 2011 and 2012.

What You Should Know

- The Sounders averaged 44,038 fans per home game in 2013. That total was nearly double the next-highest in Major League Soccer. The Galaxy ranked second with an average of 22,152.

- Sigi Schmid was the only Seattle coach until Brian Schmetzer took over in 2016. Schmid previously coached the Galaxy and the Columbus Crew SC. He won the most regular season matches in MLS history with 228. But only Schmetzer coached the Sounders to a league title.

- The Sounders are a rare MLS franchise without a team mascot.

- The original Seattle soccer franchise played in the North American Soccer League. The Sounders of that league twice played for the championship. But they lost in 1977 and 1982 to the New York Cosmos.

- The first player signed by the Sounders was Sebastien Le Toux in 2008. He had been named Most Valuable Player of the United Soccer League the previous year. But Le Toux scored just one goal for Seattle in 2009 before leaving to star for other teams.

- A Seattle soccer fan club numbered just 30 members before the Sounders were given an MLS franchise. The Emerald City Supporters soon grew to 2,000 members.

- The Sounders run a minor league team called the Sounders FC 2. They play in the United Soccer League. Their top talent is groomed for promotion to the MLS team.

- Fredy Montero has scored the most goals for the Sounders in five of their first eight MLS years. But Obafemi Martins owns the single-season team record with 19 goals scored in 2014.

- Among the Sounders owners is Paul Allen. Allen also owns the NFL Seattle Seahawks and NBA Portland Trail Blazers.

- Sounders goalkeeper Kasey Keller was nearly 42 years old when he played his last match for the team in 2011.

- CenturyLink Field is not just the home of the Sounders. The Seahawks also play their football games there.

Quick Stats

2009: Wins U.S. Open Cup title
2010: Captures another U.S. Open Cup
2011: Takes third straight U.S. Open Cup
2012: Reaches Western Conference finals
2014: Earns Supporters' Shield
2014: Earns spot in Western Conference finals
2016: Wins first MLS crown

2009
Sounders defeat New York in MLS debut behind two goals and an assist from Fredi Montero; victory over D.C. United gives Sounders U.S. Open Cup title.

2010
Sounders capture second straight U.S. Open Cup with defeat of Columbus Crew SC.

2011
Win over Chicago gives Seattle third straight U.S. Open Cup crown.

2012
Shootout goal by Mario Martinez gives Sounders first trip to Western Conference finals.

2013
Nearly 70,000 fans arrive at CenturyLink Field to watch Seattle defeat the Portland Timbers.

2014
Sounders complete Supporters' Shield season with 2-0 victory over Galaxy; tie against Dallas gives Sounders berth in Western Conference finals.

2015
Defeat in penalty kicks against Dallas knocks Seattle out of playoffs.

2016
Shootout goal by Roman Torres clinches win over Toronto and first MLS title for Sounders.

Glossary

adapt
A change to make life better or easier

attendance
The number of fans at an event

bye
Earning the right to not play a round in the playoffs

Colombian
Person from the South American country of Colombia

diversity
Different kinds of people

dynasty
A run of championships by a sports team

expansion
New franchise given to a city in a sports league

franchise
A sports organization that features a team

international
Anything to do with more than one country

interpreter
Person that allows people speaking two different languages understand each other

MLS Cup
The championship match in Major League Soccer

playoffs
Series of sports games or matches held after the regular season to determine a champion

Puget Sound
Body of water along the coast of Washington State

rivalries
Higher level of competitive fire between teams

shootout
A series of shots on goal to determine the winner of a tied soccer match

Further Reading

Latham, Andrew. *Soccer Smarts for Kids: 60 Skills, Strategies, and Secrets.* Emeryville, CA: Rockridge Press, 2016.

Roth, B. A. *David Beckham: Born to Play.* New York, New York: Grosset and Dunlap, 2007.

Triumph Books. *Soccer Superstars 2017.* Chicago: Triumph Books, 2017.

On the Internet

MLS Next. https://www.mlssoccer.com/next
This website details the future of Major League Soccer.

Seattle Sounders https://www.soundersfc.com/
This official Sounders site features photos, team news, and statistics.

Fredy Montero. http://www.fredymontero.co/
Visitors to this website can read about the top scorer in Sounders history and watch highlights of Montero in action.

Index

About the Author

Marty Gitlin is the author of about 120 books, mostly about sports. He won more than 45 awards during his 11 years as a newspaper sportswriter. Included was a first place for general excellence from the Associated Press. That organization also selected him as one of the top four feature writers in Ohio in 2002. Marty lives with his wife and three kids in Cleveland, Ohio.